Beyond the Baptism

BEYOND the BAPTISM

Being a Catholic Godparent

Fr. Jeffrey Kirby, STD

Our Sunday Visitor
Huntington, Indiana

Nihil Obstat
Msgr. Michael Heintz, Ph.D.
Censor Librorum

Imprimatur
✠ Kevin C. Rhoades
Bishop of Fort Wayne-South Bend
June 12, 2025

The *Nihil Obstat* and *Imprimatur* are official declarations that a book is free from doctrinal or moral error. It is not implied that those who have granted the *Nihil Obstat* and *Imprimatur* agree with the contents, opinions, or statements expressed.

30 29 28 27 26 25 1 2 3 4 5 6 7 8 9

Our Sunday Visitor Publishing Division
Our Sunday Visitor, Inc.
200 Noll Plaza
Huntington, IN 46750
www.osv.com
1-800-348-2440

ISBN: 978-1-63966-219-7 (Inventory No. T2907)
1. RELIGION—Christian Ministry—Pastoral Resources.
2. RELIGION—Christian Rituals & Practice—Sacraments.
3. RELIGION—Christianity—Catholic.

eISBN: 978-1-63966-220-3
LCCN: 2025943900

Cover and Interior design: Amanda Falk
Cover art: AdobeStock

PRINTED IN THE UNITED STATES OF AMERICA

To my padrinos,
Jose and Josie Villanueva

Contents

Introduction

So you've been asked to be a godparent! Congratulations!

But maybe you're a little unsettled because you're not exactly sure what that means. You realize that it's something more than just being a part of a baptism ceremony, but you don't know what else is expected. Well, this book is for you. In it, I'm going to walk through the role of the godparent as a ministry of faith and accompaniment. I'll explain things in an approachable way and give you some basic ideas to think about. I'll also pose some suggestions for you to do as you serve as a godparent in the life of another believer.

While this book is focused on godparents of children who are receiving infant baptism, it can also — with some prudential adjustments — be applied to godparents of those receiving adult baptism. The examples

I use throughout will refer to infants receiving baptism and their parents, but the information provided is generally applicable to any godparent.

Beyond the Baptism is meant to be a guide to help you go deeper in your ongoing call to be a godparent. This book can be helpful to you whether you are preparing to be a godparent for the first time, or are already a godparent but haven't really done anything in the life of your godchild since the baptism ceremony.

This book can also be a resource if you are a parent in the process of discerning whom to ask to serve as the godparent(s) of your child. The word *discern* is key here: As a parent, you want the best for your child; and it's essential that you seriously think and pray before choosing godparents, who should be people of strong faith with a sense of ministry and accompaniment. This book will help you to recognize the traits and qualities of people who would be supportive and faithful godparents.

Having mentioned the different uses of this book, I'd like to shift now and tell you a little bit about my own godparents and the role they've played in my life and in the life of my parents.

My *Padrinos*

In the early 1970s, my father suspected he was going to be drafted into the Unites States Army because of the Vietnam War, so he accepted the inevitable and enlisted. He was sent to Basic Combat Training, popularly known as “boot camp.” After their training, many of his fellow soldiers were sent to Vietnam. My father, however, was sent to Texas.

For a young man from the mill towns of Massachusetts and New Hampshire, Texas felt like a foreign country. He and my mother had only been married for a couple of years at that point and already had my older brother. I would come shortly afterward.

My parents were away from home; they didn’t have a car, money was tight, and the demands of life were overwhelming. My father was trying to find a balance between his life as a soldier and his life as a husband and father. In this arena, a very providential man came into his life. My father’s platoon sergeant, Jose Villanueva, was a no-nonsense kind of man. He took my father under his wing and showed him the way. He taught my father how to pursue excellence in the motor pool and in the home. By extension, his wife, Josie, became fast friends with and a maternal mentor to my mother, who was away from her own mother and aunts.

When the time came for my baptism, it was obvious to my parents whom they would ask to serve as my godparents: Jose and Josie, who readily agreed. Back then, I only knew them by the Spanish word for godparents. They were (and are) my *padrinos.*

The couple took this responsibility seriously. One of my earliest photos is of Jose holding me shortly after my baptism. Throughout my early life, he and Josie sent me Christmas cards and birthday gifts.

Since my *padrinos* were Mexican American, they introduced me to different traditions and customs of our universal Church. For example, I was probably the only Irish American kid in my community who walked and sang the *Las Posadas* every Christmas. The nine-day custom traces the journey of the Holy Family as they searched for housing and were rejected and dismissed. Every evening would conclude with the *aguinaldos*, a small bag of candy and sweets. This was a beloved tradition of my godparents, and they generously shared it with me.

In addition, the first image of Our Lady that I knew (and the go-to for my entire life) is Our Lady of Guadalupe. My *padrinos* had a huge picture of her in their living room. In my early mind, that's what Mary looked like!

Throughout my life, my godparents have kept in touch with me and my parents. It was a great honor to have my godfather serve as one of the lectors at my First Mass after my priestly ordination. And it was immensely consoling to see Jose and Josie reach out to and minister to my mother after my father's passing.

My godparents have always been there as a spiritual and encouraging presence.

I share some of these memories because I recognize that my experience of what it means to have godparents has been exemplary. It's my great hope that all baptized Christians will have similar experiences with their own godparents.

Being a godparent is about faith and accompaniment. In the case of infant baptism, it's about collaborating with Christian parents and seeking to be involved in the human and spiritual development of a precious child. Being a godparent should not be taken lightly. It is a sacred trust. It is a sacred duty. That's where this book comes in.

A Resource and Help to You

The task of being a godparent and sharing a ministry of accompaniment to another is a responsibility that requires attentiveness, creativity, and great faith. This book is meant as a resource and help to you, a new, or soon-to-be-new, godparent. In addition to learning what this ministry entails, you will also come away from this book with a strong sense that the responsibilities of a godparent are achievable and can even be fun!

In each chapter of this book, you'll find a teaching on an essential part of baptism and what it means to be a godparent (presented in a casual way with pastoral stories to help develop important points); a summary of main points; a collection of spiritual resources and practices; and a list of some possible activities that can help you live your call as a godparent more fully.

Chapter One

The Sacred Actions of Baptism

Have mercy on me, O God,
according to thy steadfast love;
according to thy abundant mercy
blot out my transgressions.
Wash me thoroughly from my iniquity,
and cleanse me from my sin!

— *Psalm 51:1–2*

A few years ago, a young couple asked to meet with me to talk about baptism. When they arrived for our meeting, they were carrying a baby, so I knew where the conversation was heading. The couple introduced themselves and explained that they were new to the area and had recently had their first child.

I congratulated and welcomed them.

After the pleasantries, the couple told me they were upset because someone from my parish staff had told them that in order to have their baby baptized, the family needed to be registered parishioners and actively living the Faith. The couple explained that they were happy to register but were angry because they felt they were being "judged."

The couple told me they were not attending Sunday Mass or actively living out some other aspects of the Faith. In light of this, following my guidance, the staff had let them know they needed to be on a pastoral plan for several months to show they were living the Faith and were active members of the parish before their baby could be baptized.

"How can anyone judge us?" they asked. "And we have family who want to come for the baby's baptism!"

Without realizing it, the couple was making two very different points; I started with the first. "No one is judging you," I told them. "Right now, you're not living the Faith, and during the baptism you'll be asked to commit yourself before God to passing on the Faith to your child. The pastoral plan isn't a punishment. It's meant to help you to live the Faith and be ready to make the commitments required of you at your baby's baptism."

My response only frustrated them more. "How can you do this?" they asked me. "Everyone is waiting for the baptism. Both of our families want to come."

The husband pointed to his wife. "And her grandmother is a living saint. She needs to see this baptism, and she isn't getting any younger."

I attempted to let peace rule the day as I responded, "Yes, it's important that families come and share in the sacred moment of your baby's baptism. However, baptism isn't principally about a family gathering. Baptism is about your child becoming a member of God's family. We want God to be a part of the baptism. And if the baptism is going to be what it's meant to be, then we need to make sure that you are as prepared as possible to pass on the Faith."

The conversation continued in circular motion. The young couple remained upset because they would not be getting the family gathering they wanted. Sadly, this particular meeting did not end well. (Yet thanks be to God, as a pastor I have had many similar conversations that have led to deeper conversion and an authentic return to the practice of the Faith.)

In this conversation, the battle wasn't between a priest and a young couple. The dispute was over the purpose of baptism, and that's why I share this story here. In its popular understanding, baptism has become a mere welcoming ceremony or family celebration with little or no acknowledgment of God's presence and action. There are no expectations of faith or discipleship on the part of either the parents or godparents.

In such a context, being a godparent in particular is viewed as simply an honorary gesture for family members, close friends, or loved ones of the parents. There is no expectation that godparents will help nurture the faith of their godchildren or give witness to the Gospel. In this expression of baptism, the sacrament is radically secularized, and its spiritual purpose eclipsed by tribalism and sentimentalism.

This view of baptism is tragically minimalistic and deprives the child, parents, godparents, extended family, and local parish of an opportunity to celebrate and rejoice over God's presence in their midst.

In reality, baptism is not a celebration of one's extended family or some type of a cultural ceremony; rather, it is a graced sacramental action of God in the midst of his people. In baptism, God is bringing about a mighty deed of deliverance and redemption. Baptism is about the entire family of God (not just one immediate family) witnessing the power of God to bring forth eternal life in the soul of the baptized person. Baptism is about grace, faith, discipleship, and witness. Baptism is about the presence of God and the things of God.

Baptism makes no sense without God and the workings of his grace.

If you are a godparent or preparing to become one, you must have a strong understanding of what baptism truly is and what it does. In response to the trends of secularism, we are called to charitably and gently hold the line and point humanity (which includes young parents) to the sacred actions of baptism and lead them to rejoice at the marvels and majesty of God.

Our Own Baptism

Like most Catholic Christians, I was baptized when I was very young. I don't remember the sacramental celebration. I only know of it because of pictures, stories, and my baptismal certificate that has followed me through life.

As a pastor, I try to celebrate the baptisms of my parish during the Sunday Mass whenever possible. Before the baptism, I call all the children up so they can stand by the baptismal font and see what a baptism looks like. While the children will not be able to remember their own baptisms, witnessing one will give them memories of what a baptism looks like, and hopefully some sense of why this sacrament is so important. Such a public celebration of baptism is also a reminder to adult Christians of how sacred baptism is and what God does in a person's soul at baptism.

Since many of us were baptized as infants, it's easy for us to overlook or not be aware of the powerful things God accomplished in our souls at our baptism. Thus, watching the baptisms of others and reviewing what exactly happens at baptism can be very helpful for our own spiritual growth. This is important for every Christian, but it's particularly important for Christian parents and godparents, since they will need to teach these lessons to young believers as they grow in the Faith.

In baptism, God brings about certain objective, supernatural effects within us. These divine effects then inspire some specific, personal, subjective responses from us.

As we try to understand baptism, let's start with the objective, supernatural actions of God. Through baptism, God removes all our sin and begins his saving work within us. The Church teaches that all men are affected by the wound of original sin. As the *Catechism of the Catholic Church* expresses it, "By yielding to the tempter, Adam and Eve committed a *personal sin*, but this sin affected *the human nature* that they would then transmit *in a fallen state*" (404).

Saint Peter declared this truth in his sermon at the first Pentecost: "Peter said to them, 'Repent, and be baptized every one of you in the name of Jesus Christ so that your sins may be forgiven; and you will receive the gift of the Holy Spirit'" (Acts 2:38). In baptism, we are taken from the death of sin and brought into the abundant life of grace.

In our baptism, God the Father says to each of us exactly what he said to the Lord Jesus: "This is my Son, the Beloved, with whom I am well pleased" (Mt 3:17). In baptism, therefore, we become adopted children of God. We become children by grace. Saint Paul describes this process:

> But when the fullness of time had come, God sent his Son, born of a woman, born under the law, in order to redeem those who were under the law, so that we might receive adoption as children. And because you are children, God has sent the Spirit of his Son into our hearts,

> crying, "Abba! Father!" So you are no longer a slave but a child, and if a child then also an heir, through God. (Galatians 4:4–7)

In giving us new life in baptism, the objective and supernatural actions of God include the removal of our sins, our adoption into his family, the giving of the Holy Spirit, and a welcoming into the Church, the Body of Christ.

Saint Paul beautifully summarizes these actions of God:

> I therefore, the prisoner in the Lord, beg you to lead a life worthy of the calling to which you have been called, with all humility and gentleness, with patience, bearing with one another in love, making every effort to maintain the unity of the Spirit in the bond of peace. There is one body and one Spirit, just as you were called to the one hope of your calling, one Lord, one faith, one baptism, one God and Father of all, who is above all and through all and in all. (Ephesians 4:1–6)

In baptism, the Lord Jesus chose us and brought us to the Father. The Lord Jesus tells us: "You did not choose me but I chose you. And I appointed you to go and bear fruit, fruit that will last, so that the Father will give you whatever you ask him in my name" (Jn 15:16). In this way, we can see that the work of our redemption was initiated by the Lord Jesus. This is a humbling reality. He chose us and calls us to himself.

Incidentally, this is one of the reasons why the Church has always been comfortable with baptizing infants. Baptism is first and foremost the initiative of God.

Throughout his apostolic letters, Saint Paul gives us a developed theology of baptism. He tells us that baptism is the new circumcision:

> In him also you were circumcised with a spiritual circumcision, by putting off the body of the flesh in the circumcision of Christ; when you were buried with him in baptism, you were also raised with him through faith in the power of God, who raised him from the dead. (Colossians 2:11–12)

In the Old Covenant, circumcision was performed on the eighth day of a male child's life outside of the womb. The circumcision was the bodily mark that indicated that he was a member of the Chosen People. In the New Covenant, the sign that someone belongs to God's people is baptism and the presence of the Holy Spirit in them.

We receive our status as a chosen son or daughter through the waters of baptism. And just as in Judaism circumcision was done early in the child's life, so the Church today is comfortable with baptizing infants. The focus is always on the action of God. No one chooses themselves to be in the Chosen People. We are chosen by God in baptism. He is the one who inaugurates a relationship with us in the midst of his people.

By being adopted by God the Father in the name of Jesus Christ, we enter into the communion of the Holy Trinity. We can honestly call God our Father, the Lord Jesus our Older Brother, and the Holy Spirit our Companion. It is this familial relationship that allows us to come before God, offer our lives and prayers to him, and trust in his love and providential care for us.

This saving action of God is not carried out in a vacuum. Through baptism, we become members of the Church, the Body of Christ. We enter into communion with the Lord Jesus and with every other baptized person. In baptism, we are made one. We become siblings to Jesus Christ and siblings to one another.

> For just as the body is one and has many members, and all the members of the body, though many, are one body, so it is with Christ. For in the one Spirit we were all baptized into one body — Jews or Greeks, slaves or free — and we were all made to drink of one Spirit. (1 Corinthians 12:12–13)

These are the objective, supernatural actions of God. Now, let's look at the subjective, personal responses that these sacred actions call out from us.

Subjective, Personal Responses

The objective, supernatural actions of God occur with

or without our knowledge and approval. They are God acting within us. For these objective, supernatural actions of God to take root in our hearts, however, we need to rekindle them — fan them into flame — by our subjective, personal acts of faith. Saint Paul exhorts us: "For this reason I remind you to rekindle the gift of God that is within you" (2 Tm 1:6).

Once we're baptized, we need to be raised and taught in the way of the Lord Jesus by our parents, godparents, extended family, and local parish.

Sadly, this doesn't happen in many places today. The sacrament is celebrated, but often the Faith is compartmentalized and put on the proverbial shelf of a family's life. Life goes on, and the living and teaching of the Faith is forgotten.

A formation in the Faith is essential if the graces of baptism are to flourish within us. Parents, godparents, extended family, and local parishes are to take this responsibility seriously and do everything possible to provide a strong formation in the Faith. This is particularly important in the case of infant baptism. Children will rely on those entrusted with this sacred duty to teach and form them in the way of the Lord Jesus.

The *Catechism* stresses this point: "By its very nature infant Baptism requires a *post-baptismal catechumenate.* Not only is there a need for instruction after Baptism, but also for the necessary flowering of baptismal grace in personal growth. The *catechism* has its proper place here" (1231).

Baptism is not solely a sacramental ceremony or ritual; it is also a complete way of life. Baptism involves the new identity of the baptized and the Gospel mission to which all the baptized are called. Through the graces of baptism, we are invited and strengthened to accept and proclaim Jesus Christ as the Lord of our lives. Godparents have an essential role to play in accompanying their godchildren on this lifelong journey of discipleship.

Godparents, in cooperation with parents, have a sacred duty to teach the way of the Lord Jesus to their godchildren — to give them instruction, example, and mentoring in the Faith, leading them to make a personal decision for the Lord Jesus as they grow and mature (or, in the case of adult baptism, helping them to hold fast to the decision they made when they were baptized). The graces of baptism give us the faith, hope, and love necessary to make an intentional decision for the Lord Jesus and the truths of his Gospel.

Saint Peter shows us what it means to make a personal decision for Jesus Christ. He responds to Jesus' question, "Who do you say that I am?" by saying, "You are the Messiah, the Son of the living God" (Mt 16:15, 16). Saint Martha of Bethany made a similar decision for the Lord, as she demonstrated when she said: "Yes, Lord, I believe that you are the Messiah, the Son of God, the one coming into the world" (Jn 11:27).

Baptism is about choosing Jesus Christ. It is about declaring him Lord, Savior, Friend, Confidant, and

Companion. Baptism and our personal decision for Jesus Christ is about walking with him and accepting a death to our sinfulness and self-centeredness and choosing to live our lives fully for Jesus Christ.

The baptismal way of life involves us reliving the passion, death, and resurrection of the Lord Jesus every day in our own lives. We undergo the passion of temptation, fear, or anxiety. We die to these things and experience the graces of resurrection as we are given grace, hope, and confidence in Jesus Christ.

Saint Paul emphasizes this aspect of baptism:

> Do you not know that all of us who have been baptized into Christ Jesus were baptized into his death? Therefore we have been buried with him by baptism into death, so that, just as Christ was raised from the dead by the glory of the Father, so we too might walk in newness of life. (Romans 6:3–4)

By understanding baptism from the personal, subjective perspective, we realize that the grace of conversion has been given to us at baptism, and that grace compels us to an ongoing process of renewal every day as we seek to live the baptismal way of life and faithfully follow the way of the Lord Jesus. The call to conversion is constant. It begins at baptism and continues throughout our lives as we reject sin and choose Jesus Christ.

At the same time, we are not meant to live this

call to conversion alone. The Church in her wisdom provides godparents to help the baptized choose Jesus Christ again and again, through the highs and lows of life. Godparents remind us of our place in the Body of Christ, encouraging us to live by Jesus' most excellent way of love and to adhere to a new standard of being. This new standard includes everything we do, from how we show mercy, to our care for the poor and sick, to the treatment of our bodies, to how we spend money, and to every other action — however important or trivial — in this life. Our baptism is about a constant dying to self in the service of Jesus Christ and being an active part of his ongoing saving mission in our world.

Saint Paul gives us great encouragement as he reflects on the results of living by God's grace and seeking to be with the Lord at all times: "For through the law I died to the law, so that I might live to God. I have been crucified with Christ; and it is no longer I who live, but it is Christ who lives in me. And the life I now live in the flesh I live by faith in the Son of God, who loved me and gave himself for me" (Gal 2:19–20).

While the objective actions of baptism cannot be overlooked, so the subjective aspects of the sacrament cannot be ignored either. Both are needed if the sacrament is to fulfill its purpose in the life of believers and in the Church.

The movement of God calls out for our response of faith and acceptance of our new life in Jesus Christ. It is a tragedy when someone has been purified of sin, adopted by God, and made a member of the Body of Christ, only to avoid becoming a true friend of the Lord, refusing to follow his most excellent way of love, and failing to continue his work and invite others into his friendship. The divine initiative calls for our personal response; but we have free will, and we must freely choose it.

These are the baptismal actions and mysteries of God within the human soul and from the human soul. They are objective and subjective. They are supernatural and personal. They are the complete package of all that we are and all that we are called to be.

For godparents, this understanding of baptism is essential, both for our own continual conversion and growth, and so that we can fulfill our important role in the lives of our godchildren. Our very identity as godparents flows from the reality of what baptism is and what it does in the individual soul and in the life of the Church.

Key Takeaways

- ➡ Baptism is the beginning of our relationship with God — a relationship that God himself initiates.
- ➡ Baptism involves objective, supernatural actions by God, which include the removal of our sins, our adoption into his family, the giving of the Holy Spirit, and a welcoming

into the Church, the Body of Christ.

➡ In order for the objective, supernatural actions to flourish within us, we need to receive instruction and guidance in the way of the Lord Jesus — this is where the role of Christian godparents is critical.

➡ Our subjective, personal actions include making a personal decision for Jesus Christ, living the baptismal way of life, rejecting sin, and seeking to live by virtue and holiness in an ongoing, lifelong process of conversion.

Spiritual Resources and Practices

As a godparent, you will need to find ways to teach the Faith, accompany your godchild in the ways of faith, and share a strong witness to the Lord Jesus. To help you get started, at the end of each chapter in this book, I have included related spiritual resources and practices to help you grow in your own faith and support the faith of your godchild.

- Read the accounts of the baptism of the Lord Jesus: Matthew 3:13–17, Mark 1:9–11, Luke 3:21–22, and John 1:29–34.
- Spend some time reflecting on the six baptismal promises. These are the promises

you made at your own baptism and witnessed at the baptism of your godchild. With these promises, you renounced Satan, all his works, and all his empty promises. And you professed belief in God, the Father Almighty, Creator of heaven and earth; in Jesus Christ, his only Son, our Lord; and in the Holy Spirit, the holy Catholic Church, the communion of saints, the forgiveness of sins, the resurrection of the body, and life everlasting.

- Study the portion of the *Catechism of the Catholic Church* on baptism (1213–1284) and the ways of prayer (2700–2724).
- Read a strong spiritual book on the life of the Lord Jesus. There are many wonderful books on this topic, such as Pope Benedict XVI's classic three-volume work *Jesus of Nazareth* and Romano Guardini's *The Lord*. For more contemporary resources, consider *The Life of Jesus Christ: Understanding the Story of the Gospels* by Russell Shaw and *A Life of Conversion: Meeting Christ in the Gospel* by Derek Rotty.

Pray the following prayers for your godchild:

The ***Suscipe*** *Prayer of St. Ignatius of Loyola*

Take, Lord, and receive all my liberty,
my memory, my understanding,
and my entire will,
all I have and call my own.
You have given all to me.
To you, Lord, I return it.
Everything is yours; do with it what you will.
Give me only your love and your grace,
that is enough for me.

The ***Memorare*** *to the Blessed Virgin Mary*

Remember, O most gracious Virgin Mary, that never was it known that anyone who fled to thy protection, implored thy help, or sought thy intercession, was left unaided. Inspired by this confidence I fly unto thee, O Virgin of virgins, my Mother. To thee do I come, before thee I stand, sinful and sorrowful. O Mother of the Word Incarnate, despise not my petitions, but in thy mercy hear and answer me. Amen.

Guardian Angel Prayer

Angel of God, my guardian dear,
to whom God's love commits me here,
ever this day be at my side,
to light and guard, to rule and guide. Amen.

Possible Activities*

- Remember your godchild during the Mass of the Lord's Baptism, which is celebrated on the Sunday after the feast of the Epiphany. If age appropriate, renew the baptismal promises with your godchild either in person or by phone on the solemnity.
- Celebrate the anniversary of your godchild's baptism. Go to Mass or Adoration and pray for your godchild on that day. Reach out to your godchild with a phone call, a card, or a gift, which can be a wonderful gesture and yearly reminder of this important anniversary.
- Send your godchild a small, faith-based gift for Christmas.

* All suggested activities here and elsewhere in this book should be carried out in collaboration with your godchild's parents. The directives of the Church's Safe Environment policies should always guide how you minister and accompany your godchild. Each suggestion must also be discerned and adjusted to the age and maturity of your godchild.

Chapter Two

A Binding Promise and Sacred Trust

What shall I return to the Lord
for all his bounty to me?
I will lift up the cup of salvation
and call on the name of the Lord,
I will pay my vows to the Lord
in the presence of all his people.

— *Psalm 116:12–14*

Early in my priesthood, I worked with a couple as they prepared for marriage. They seemed like sincere disciples who were trying to know the Lord Jesus better and understand what it meant to be called together in holy matrimony by God. The preparation went well. They answered questions, read assignments, and engaged in serious conversation. I saw them at Sunday Mass. Everything appeared to be in order.

At last it was time for this couple to get married. The Mass was well planned, and it was a beautiful liturgy with a moving exchange of vows. Since I had gotten to know the couple so well, I made arrangements to attend the reception afterward.

Toward the end of the evening, as I prepared to leave, I went to find the couple to express my congratulations and farewell. The groom was easy to find, but it took me a little searching to find the bride. Finally, I spotted her. As I approached, she stood with her back to me, talking to a friend.

Neither woman could see me, but I heard the friend say to her, "This is a huge step. I can't believe you're married!"

The bride responded, "Yeah, we're giving it a shot!" Then she laughed and said, "If it goes south, we can always get a divorce."

My heart sank.

As the bride made this comment, her friend saw me, and her face said it all. The bride realized something was wrong and turned. When she saw me, there was instant shock, and then she tried to bounce back "Father! It's good to see you. Thank you so much for coming."

"Yes," I responded, "it was good to be with you." And then, from my soul, I began to speak before I knew it:

"Divorce is not an option. Make sure you believe in love."

"Oh, Father, I was just joking," the bride responded and gave me a hug. I smiled and wished her the best.

As I walked to my car, my heart was deeply troubled. Who jokes about divorce? Was she really joking? Did she understand what she had just done at the altar of God?

Of course, I sincerely hope it was just a bad joke, and I keep this couple in my prayers. But I share this troubling story as an example of a broader cultural problem. Our approach to commitment as a society is fickle. We can make vows and promises, even before God, and then treat them very cheaply.

As Christians, we need to be the difference. We need to take seriously what we say. We need to be accountable to the vows and promises we make, which begins with the promises of our baptism — promises that are witnessed to by parents and godparents in the case of infant baptism.

Here's a different story that can give hope about our ability to keep our promises, particularly for those of us who are godparents.

While I was a student-priest in Rome, I would give tours to different groups. On one occasion, I was leading a group from the various military bases in Italy. They only had a few hours, and our goal was to see as much of the Eternal City as possible. There was one soldier, however, who had bought a small rosary. He told me it was for his godchild and that he wanted to mail it from the Vatican post office.

I warned the soldier that it would be complicated to mail something from the Vatican. We were on the other side of the city, and he would have to take a taxi to get to the post office. He would miss the majority of the tour. The soldier was undaunted. He knew what he needed to do. So I directed him to the local taxi stand, told him what to say in Italian, and drew directions to the Vatican post office on the back of a sheet a paper. I also told him how he would need to package the rosary. During this entire process, the soldier was attentive to every detail and overwhelmingly grateful. Finally, I told him where we would be and how to find us when he was finished. I stressed that he had to be on time since a bus was meeting us at that location.

When we arrived at our rally point a few hours later, the soldier was sitting there, waiting for us with a huge smile on his face. He told me everything had gone smoothly, and the package was in the mail. The soldier missed seeing most of Rome, but he didn't care. He wanted his godchild to receive a rosary from Rome in an envelope with a Vatican postmark, and he made that happen. The joy of this committed godfather was palpable.

This is an example of a person who made a promise before God to serve as a godparent and who took his sacred duty seriously.

Our words have power. When we speak words to praise God, we show our fullest selves as human beings. When we speak words to make vows or promises, we bind ourselves in a unique way to God and to another person. As we fulfill those vows and promises, we become more of who we are meant to be, fulfilling our sacred duties and giving ourselves in service to another.

Words are not meant to be cheap. They are meant to be rich in love and purpose.

Do we consider the promises of parents and godparents at baptism to be mere formalities? Perhaps our understanding of these promises may be overly casual and merely ceremonial. But make no mistake: These are promises made to God, and he takes them very seriously. In particular, he takes the promises of parents and godparents to be a sacred trust, since they involve the teaching and forming of a child to know him and follow his ways. When the baptismal promise of a parent or godparent is broken, it is chiefly the child who suffers.

With this in mind, let's talk about the promise that a godparent makes to God and what that means in the life of faith of both the godparent and the godchild.

The Church's Directives

Whenever a person is asked to be a godparent, there are two parties giving the invitation. The immediate party is the Christian father and mother. The principal party is God, with his angels and saints. When you were asked to be a godparent, it wasn't just the child's father or mother making the request. It was God in his providence asking you to help the parents to raise their child in the practice of the Faith.

We cannot lose sight of the realization of God's providence and the part God plays in the selection of a godparent. You have not become a godparent by accident or coincidence. Your selection has been an act of divine providence. God has a plan for your godchild, and *you* are a part of that plan.

We can identify three movements that led to your service as a godparent.

The first consists of the formal directives of the Church. The second is the discernment and selection by the Christian parents. The third is your discernment and decision after being invited to serve as a godparent.

Let's review the formal directives of the Church first.

The Code of Canon Law is the collection of all the ordinances that govern and guide the life of the Church. As we examine the formal directives of the Church on godparents, we need to turn to Canons 872–874. These canons will teach us what the Church expects in her godparents.

From this collection of canons, we can draw the following applications:

- The person to be baptized is only required to have one godparent. If there is a custom of having two godparents, then two may be chosen. If there are two, then it must be one man and one woman. Two godparents of the same sex are not permitted. It is not required that the two godparents be married.

- The mother or the father of the baptized person may not serve as the godparent. A godparent's responsibility is to assist the parents in the Christian formation of the baptized person. The two roles are interrelated but distinct.
- A godparent must be at least sixteen years of age and have the proper aptitude and intention to be a godparent.
- A godparent must have received the Sacrament of Confirmation.
- A godparent must be a Catholic in good standing, actively living the Faith and taking his or her own discipleship seriously.
- A non-Catholic Christian cannot serve as a godparent. The non-Catholic Christian can be present as a Christian witness so long as a godparent is present.
- A Catholic who is married outside the Church, or who is cohabitating outside of the Sacrament of Matrimony, is not permitted to serve as a godparent due to the irregular nature of such a lifestyle.
- Any Catholic who is not living according to the doctrine of the Church or who is manifestly at odds with central teachings of the Church cannot serve as a godparent.

These are the formal directives of the Church regarding godparents. They are obligatory when it comes to the selection of a godparent. Some of these directives might unsettle parents or perhaps make the selection of a godparent more difficult. Such situations might cause frustration. Rather than seeing these directives as some type of cold law that is imposed upon us or as distant rules that restrict what we want, however, we can view them as the pastoral guidance of the Church, who wants the best for a newly baptized person.

It is not an easy task to serve as a godparent. One must be personally committed to following Christ as a disciple before trying to give a faithful witness and provide authentic formation to a newly baptized person. The formal directives of the Church are thus meant to be a help to Christian parents. They set the bar high and show parents the type of believer they should look for in their search for a godparent for their child.

The Discernment of Christian Parents

Christian parents should take the selection of a godparent for their child very seriously.

The Church entrusts the right and duty of selecting a godparent to the parents of the child. The parents have the solemn responsibility to scan and search the body of believers for a godparent who is worthy and ready to help them raise and form a new Christian. With this understanding, Christian parents begin their discernment.

In the spiritual tradition of the Church, when we speak of discernment, we are referring to a process of prayer, spiritual observation, examination of a situation, and a scrutiny of ourselves and others. The word *discernment* comes from the same Greek word that gives us the word *diagnosis*. Think of a time when you went to your doctor's office, and he asked you about your general health, specific symptoms, and the frequency and severity of symptoms. The doctor was going through this process so he could find a cause of your illness. He was discerning.

The goal of discernment is not simply to identify a spiritual illness, although recognizing a spiritual illness can be a helpful part of the process. Discernment is mainly about searching for God's will. Our prayer, observations, examination, and scrutinies are all in service to the task of seeing and accepting God's will.

In light of this goal, the *Catechism* teaches us: "The beatitude of heaven sets the standards for discernment in the use of earthly goods in keeping with the law of God" (1729). Let's stress the point: The goal of discernment is to discover God's will. This means that, ultimately, the goal of discernment is to order everything in our lives so that we, and those under our care, might get to heaven.

As Christians, we are called to discern all the time. We discern our general vocations as Christians (married life, consecrated service). We discern specifics within our vocation (whom to marry, where to serve). We discern our talents and abilities. We discern our profession and opportunities relating to employment. Married couples discern the planning of their families. Parish priests discern where to push and where to pull in the life of their parishes. The list is endless. We are a discerning people. We want to do what God is asking of us. The Christian way of life is about discernment because it is all about living for God and according to his will.

The selection of a godparent also involves discernment.

Choosing a godparent is not simply looking at extended family members and saying, "Yeah, Uncle George would be great," or selecting someone as an honor or so they don't feel left out ("It would mean a lot to Sally if we asked her"). While family ties and affection have their place, these need to be secondary to the first consideration: Who is going to be the best witness to the Faith and a help to us in raising this child as a Christian believer?

Such a provocative question compels Christian parents to pray. They should approach God with empty hands, commend their child to him, and ask the Holy Spirit to lead them in finding the right godparent for their child. In such a process, it shouldn't overly surprise Christian parents if the Holy Spirit directs them to someone they may not have initially thought of or even considered!

In addition to prayer, Christian parents are called to spiritual observation. The formal directives can help parents in this observation. While no one can judge the heart of another, we can watch and see how a person lives and what fruits a person's soul is producing. The Lord Jesus taught us:

> Beware of false prophets, who come to you in sheep's clothing but inwardly are ravenous wolves. You will know them by their fruits. Are grapes gathered from thorns, or figs from thistles? In the same way, every good tree bears good fruit, but the bad tree bears bad fruit. A good tree cannot bear bad fruit, nor can a bad tree bear good fruit. Every tree that does not bear good fruit is cut down and thrown into the fire. Thus you will know them by their fruits. (Matthew 7:15–20)

And so, in seeking the best godparent for their child, Christian parents must look at a person's life. Some questions are easy to answer: Is this person's marriage in good standing with the Church? Does he go to Mass on Sundays and holy days of obligation? Is she actively involved in the life of her parish? Does he pray? Is she a person of service?

In addition to these questions, Christian parents need to be willing to go deeper, assessing with honesty (and without rash judgment). Has the process of conversion really begun in this prospective godparent's own heart?

How can we tell if conversion has begun in a soul? When conversion has begun, a person will bear the fruits of God's Spirit. As a help, Saint Paul teaches us about these fruits:

> By contrast, the fruit of the Spirit is love, joy, peace, patience, kindness, generosity, faithfulness, gentleness, and self-control. There is no law against such things. And those who belong to Christ Jesus have crucified the flesh with its passions and desires. If we live by the Spirit, let us also be guided by the Spirit. Let us not become conceited, competing against one another, envying one another. (Galatians 5:22–26)

Drawing from the Apostle's other writings, the Church expands the list and provides a fuller summary:

> The *fruits* of the Spirit are perfections that the Holy Spirit forms in us as the first fruits of eternal glory. The tradition of the Church lists twelve of them: "charity, joy, peace, patience, kindness, goodness, generosity, gentleness, faithfulness, modesty, self-control, chastity." (CCC 1832)

As Christian parents observe people who might serve as their child's godparents, they should actively look for these fruits of God's Spirit in their lives.

After prayer and spiritual observation, parents must be honest with themselves and make sure that prospective godparents are being considered for the right reasons. In our lives and discernment, the *Catechism* reminds us that we are fallen:

> The doctrine of original sin, closely connected with that of redemption by Christ, provides lucid discernment of man's situation and activity in the world. By our first parents' sin, the devil has acquired a certain domination over man, even though man remains free. Original sin entails "captivity under the power of him who thenceforth had the power of death, that is, the devil." Ignorance of the fact that man has a wounded nature inclined to evil gives rise to serious errors in the areas of education, politics, social action, and morals. (407)

We are easily swayed by what is easy and more enjoyable. We can make decisions based on vanity, acceptance, and respectability. We can cave to the ego and emotional wants of others. Parents need to be aware of this and willing to walk through a strong examination of conscience and a scrutiny of their own hearts before asking someone to serve as godparent for their child.

The only real question still stands: Are the prospective godparents being chosen because of their faith and their capacity to help teach and form a new Christian in the way of the Lord Jesus?

Once the Christian parents select a possible godparent, they should reach out and talk with the person. This should not be done casually, but given time and gravitas. Perhaps the Christian parents could invite the person over for dinner or schedule a time to sit down and talk. This approach allows the parents to explain how seriously they take the role of the godparent and the hopes they have of the godparent being a part of their child's life for the long haul. These expectations need to be voiced, as while they are the true standard for godparents, they are extremely uncommon.

After parents have spoken to someone about serving as a godparent, that believer is led to discernment: Is God asking me to serve this family and child in this way? Am I able to take on this responsibility in my life right now? Can I fulfill the sacred duties of being a godparent?

The Discernment of the Prospective Godparent

After reviewing the formal directives of the Church and the discernment of Christian parents, we now turn to the prospective godparent's discernment. Even if you have already accepted the invitation to serve as a godparent, or have been a godparent for many years, you can walk through the discernment process retrospectively. You might be surprised to find that doing so can still assist you in understanding what you have undertaken and how you can live your call.

Even if the invitation to serve as a godparent appears random, it is not random in God's eyes. The providence of God is the mover of all things. Our task is to discern and seek an answer to the question: Is God asking me to serve in this way right now?

It's easy to be honored and humbled by the invitation to be a godparent, but these are not sufficient reasons for accepting the responsibility. The focus isn't our ego, but the training and formation of a child in the way of the Lord Jesus. And so, just as Christian parents must walk through the discernment process, so must the prospective godparent. This process requires prayer, spiritual observation, and personal examination and scrutiny.

If you are discerning whether to serve as a godparent, you need to be honest in your own heart. This discernment requires freedom — the ability to say yes or no. In this discernment process, you will need to take time to pray and reflect on these important questions: Where do I stand with the Lord Jesus? Where do the Christian parents and the family that has invited me to be a godparent stand with the Lord?

This discernment begins with an evaluation of your own discipleship. While we are all works in progress, if we are called to guide and form another in the way of the Lord, we must possess some level of growth ourselves.

Recall the powerful account of Saint Peter and the man who was lame from birth:

> One day Peter and John were going up to the temple at the hour of prayer, at three o'clock in the afternoon. And a man lame from birth was being carried in. People would lay him daily at the gate of the temple called the Beautiful Gate

> so that he could ask for alms from those entering the temple. When he saw Peter and John about to go into the temple, he asked them for alms. Peter looked intently at him, as did John, and said, "Look at us." And he fixed his attention on them, expecting to receive something from them. But Peter said, "I have no silver or gold, but what I have I give you; in the name of Jesus Christ of Nazareth, stand up and walk." And he took him by the right hand and raised him up; and immediately his feet and ankles were made strong. Jumping up, he stood and began to walk, and he entered the temple with them, walking and leaping and praising God. (Acts of the Apostles 3:1–8)

While there are many lessons that can be drawn from this account, let's focus on what Saint Peter said: "I have no silver or gold, but what I have I give you."

In discipleship, we can only give what we have. It is important to be transparent with ourselves and to acknowledge our strengths and weaknesses. As you discern the offer to serve as a godparent, make sure you have something to give.

Every call to mission is first and foremost a call to greater discipleship. Accepting the call to be a godparent is a summons from the Lord Jesus to go deeper and to surrender more of ourselves to him. Serving as a godparent is a profound ministry in the life of the Church.

If your faith makes you ready, then you may confidently accept the invitation and seek to serve as a godparent with vigor and zeal for the Lord and his Gospel.

As you discern your own discipleship, you must also assess where the Christian parents are in their faith and discipleship. You will need to have a sober realization of what variations of service might be asked of you as you serve as a godparent to this particular family and its needs.

In addition, it's important to take time to evaluate again what it means to make a promise to God and asses the specific promise you will make as a godparent.

In the story I shared earlier, the soldier I met in Rome understood his promise to be a godparent. Sadly, this is not always the case. In our society, we often approach promises, even those made to God, in an overly relaxed and minimalized fashion. We say things and then life goes on. Promises are made, and promises are broken.

This cannot be our approach to promises as Christian disciples. The Christian believer is called to live a life of integrity and faithfulness, and godparents need to witness to this reality by their own example. A godparent makes a promise before God to assist the parents in forming the newly baptized in the way of the Lord. (In the case of adult baptism, the godparent promises to assist the newly baptized in growing as a faithful disciple.)

Let's look at the moment in the baptismal rite when this promise is made:

CELEBRANT: You have asked to have your child

> baptized. In doing so you are accepting the responsibility of training him (her) in the practice of the faith. It will be your duty to bring him (her) up to keep God's commandments as Christ taught us, by loving God and our neighbor. Do you clearly understand what you are undertaking?
>
> PARENTS: **We do.**
>
> CELEBRANT: [to the godparent(s)] Are you ready to help the parents of this child in their duty as Christian parents?
>
> GODPARENTS: **We are.**

Admittedly, you have to pay attention to the rite, or you might miss it. But there it is: The godparents are asked if they are ready to help the Christian parents fulfill their duty. In other words, each godparent is asked, "Do you agree to carry this responsibility with these Christian parents? Will you be a Simon of Cyrene to the parents of this child and help them to carry whatever crosses might come with raising this child as a Christian?"

Saint Paul reminds us of our call to carry one another's burdens: "Bear one another's burdens, and in this way you will fulfill the law of Christ" (Gal 6:2).

The *Catechism* stresses the important role of the godparent:

> For the grace of Baptism to unfold, the parents' help is important. So too is the role of the *godfather* and *godmother*, who must be firm believers, able and ready to help the newly baptized — child or adult — on the road of Christian life. Their task is a truly ecclesial function (*officium*). The whole ecclesial community bears some responsibility for the development and safeguarding of the grace given at Baptism. (1255)

What does the *Catechism* mean when it calls the role of the godparent an *officium*? The word literally means "office," which in theological terms refers to a sacred duty, function, or responsibility. The Church sees the godparent holding a formal place in the life of the newly baptized. There is nothing casual in the Church's approach to the function and service of the godparent.

In speaking of promises in general, the *Catechism* makes this point:

> In many circumstances, the Christian is called to make *promises* to God. Baptism and confirmation, matrimony and holy orders always entail promises. Out of personal devotion, the Christian may also promise to God this action, that prayer, this alms-giving, that pilgrimage, and so forth. Fidelity to promises made to God is a sign of the respect owed to the divine majesty and of love for a faithful God. (2101)

Our fidelity to our promises is "a sign of respect" to God's divine majesty, and it shows our gratitude for the faithfulness that God always shows us. It is a sacred duty to fulfill a promise to God. Being accountable to a promise we've made to God is an act of justice and love for him and for others. And so, making a promise before God must be weighed and considered with serious discernment.

It is a great gift and responsibility to be invited to serve as a godparent. If accepted, it is a lifelong mission given from God that compels us to give witness, to assist in the formation of a newly baptized person, and to accompany our godchild as he or she walks the way of the Lord.

Struggles Along the Way

As you discern the call to serve as a godparent, it's important to understand that you are being invited to journey through life with your godchild, and there will be ups and downs along the way. The way will be marked by joys and blessings, but also sufferings and struggles.

Here are some of the possible struggles you might encounter as a godparent, and some practical considerations for facing these challenges:

- Your godchild might live a great distance from you. Your rapport with the parents can become distant. In such instances, unless your godchild was baptized as an adult, you will have to both work on your relationship with the parents and seek to help your godchild in the ways of faith.

- You may sometimes find it difficult to fulfill the demands of your own vocation while remaining attentive to your godchild. Perhaps you have several of your own children, and they require a lot of time and attention. The idea of giving something more of yourself to a godchild can feel overwhelming. In such a scenario, do what you can. God does not ask the impossible from us. Assess your schedule and energy level and make realistic resolutions for how you can pray for and accompany your godchild.
- The family of your godchild may cease the regular practice of the Faith. You must now minister to your godchild and look for ways to encourage the family to return to a regular Mass attendance.
- The parents of your godchild might get divorced, and you might be in the fray between both parents. In such a situation, you must delicately walk the balance and see how you can help your godchild to understand what is happening and how the Faith can help.
- The parents of your godchild may not understand why you want to keep in touch and why you keep sending religious things

to their child. Hopefully, this scenario is prevented by a candid conversation in the discernment phase of being a godparent, but if not, then you will need to explain what a godparent is and what level of interaction you plan to have with their child. It is important to defer to the parents if your views differ, and in those situations, to do the best you can.

- As your godchild grows up and enters new phases of life, he or she might not want anything to do with you. In such a scenario, attempt to offer spiritual supplication and accompaniment from a respectful distance. You might be able to commiserate with your godchild's parents, since they are probably receiving a similar response from the young person.
- You may find yourself in a situation in which you have a good rapport with your godchild, and he or she wants to share something with you in confidence. If a godchild asks you not to tell his or her parents about something, be careful. Godparents are not camp counselors or life coaches. You are in service to God and the parents of your godchild. Let your godchild know that the two of you can talk, but you will share with the parents anything that influ-

ences the child's spiritual or moral health, or general well-being. Parents and godparents should always form a united front.

- You may look back and find that life has moved quickly. You agreed to be a godparent, but you've lost contact with your godchild and the family, and now you can't locate them. In this situation, you are bound to pray and make sacrifices for your godchild. It is also a noble practice to have Masses offered for your godchild.

These are some of the many possible hurdles you might face as a godparent. In each one, God will provide the wisdom and grace for you to walk through the situation and fulfill the service he has asked of you.

As you fulfill your promise to give witness to the Lord Jesus and accompany your godchild (and your godchild's family) along the way of faith, you will also experience many joys; these should also play a part in your discernment.

Joys Along the Way

The invitation to serve as a godparent carries many responsibilities, but it also brings many blessings and joys. Whenever we serve the Lord Jesus, we should look for the blessings he gives and relish the joys he bestows. Here are just a few examples of the joys that can come from serving as a godparent:

- As the years move along, you'll get to witness your godchild grow in age and faith. You'll play a part in forming the child as a disciple and see the movements of grace in his or her life.
- As a godparent, you can also see the family of your godchild deepen in their love for the Lord and his Church.
- In your ministry of accompaniment, you will hopefully be able to watch your godchild receive other sacraments, especially first holy Communion and confirmation. In some instances, you might even be asked to serve as your godchild's sponsor for confirmation.
- In tender moments, your godchild may thank you for your accompaniment and encouragement, especially during life's milestones such as middle school and high school graduation.
- In high school and college, your godchild might turn to you as a cherished mentor who can provide wisdom, counsel, and prayers.
- Your godchild might talk to you about the impact of spiritual books or gifts you have sent to help him or her to grow in a personal relationship with God.
- As your godchild grows up and your rap-

port becomes more reciprocal, your godchild might start sending books and spiritual gifts to you. In this exchange, you'll know that you helped form the habit of giving and sharing spiritual gifts in the heart of your godchild.

- You might be able to one day see your godchild enter into holy matrimony or consecrated service to the Church and know that you were a part of that journey. If you have a godson and he becomes a priest, maybe you can one day be a lector at his First Mass!

Key Takeaways

- ➡ When you were asked to be a godparent, there were two parties involved in the invitation: God and your godchild's parents.
- ➡ The Church has formal directives that guide who can serve as a godparent. These directives should guide the discernment of Christian parents on whom they will ask to serve as a godparent.
- ➡ Becoming a godparent requires discernment, both on the part of the Christian parents and on the part of the prospective godparent.
- ➡ Personal discipleship is critical to the fulfillment of the call to serve as a godparent.

➡ The promise you make as a godparent at baptism is binding. It carries a sacred duty that you are expected to fulfill to the best of your ability through the difficulties and struggles as well as the joys and blessings of life with your godchild.

Spiritual Resources and Practices

- Review some basic points of what it means to be a godparent. If possible, schedule a time to review these with the parents of your godchild. You can still do this even if the baptism is long past, and you have already been the child's godparent for some time.
- Evaluate your own discipleship and identify your strengths and areas of growth. Make resolutions to be a stronger disciple of Jesus Christ.
- On the anniversary of your godchild's baptism, review and renew the promises you and the Christian parents made to God.
- Regularly offer a decade of the Rosary for your godchild, especially on major feast days of the Church and on important anniversaries (such as your godchild's birthdays, baptism anniversaries, patron saint's feast day, and so on.). If your godchild is old enough

and available, pray the decade with him or her, whether in person or virtually.

- Walk the Stations of the Cross for your godchild, especially if he or she is undergoing difficult challenges of faith.

Pray the following prayers for your godchild:

An Act of Faith

O my God, I firmly believe
that you are one God in three divine Persons,
Father, Son, and Holy Spirit.
I believe that your divine Son became man
and died for our sins and that he will come
to judge the living and the dead.
I believe these and all the truths
which the Holy Catholic Church teaches
because you have revealed them
who are eternal truth and wisdom,
who can neither deceive nor be deceived.
In this faith I intend to live and die.
Amen.

The Salve Regina (Hail, Holy Queen)

Hail, Holy Queen, Mother of Mercy,
our life, our sweetness and our hope.

To thee do we cry,
poor banished children of Eve.
To thee do we send up our sighs,
mourning and weeping in this valley of tears.
Turn then, most gracious advocate,
thine eyes of mercy toward us,
and after this our exile,
show unto us the blessed fruit of thy womb, Jesus.
O clement, O loving,
O sweet Virgin Mary.
Amen.

Guardian Angel Prayer

Angel of God, my guardian dear,
to whom God's love commits me here,
ever this day be at my side,
to light and guard, to rule and guide.
Amen.

Possible Activities

- Look for age-appropriate Catholic periodicals and ask the parents of your godchild if you may purchase a print or digital subscription of one of them for your godchild. If they agree, subscribe to the periodical yourself as well and use the various articles and activities as a basis for conversations with your godchild.

- Look for ways to highlight liturgical seasons. For example, talk to your godchild about Lenten sacrifices and the true meaning of Easter.
- Have a Mass offered on your godchild's birthday and/or patron saint's feast day.

Chapter Three

An Extended Spiritual Family

How very good and pleasant it is
when kindred live together in unity!
It is like the precious oil on the head,
running down upon the beard,
on the beard of Aaron,
running down over the collar of his robes.

— *Psalm 133:1–2*

When I was newly ordained, I attended one of my nephew's football games. When I arrived at the game, his godmother was there with her children. They all had signs and noisemakers and were very excited about the game. Whenever there was a good play, they boisterously cheered and zealously applauded. As the game neared its end, one of the children said to me, "That's my godbrother! He plays football." She was very proud of her godbrother. I smiled and nodded. I had never heard the term "godbrother," but it made perfect sense and certainly warmed my heart.

When godparents are chosen, they become a part of their godchild's extended family. If the godparent has children, the children also share in that relationship. Wouldn't it be great if terms like *godbrother* and *godsister* became more common?

Even when they are not related by blood, it is important for godparents to see themselves as extended family members and for the parents of the godchild to welcome godparents and help them to feel included and valued.

Godparents as Extended Family Members

The Church is the family of God. This isn't a remote or poetic sentiment. The Church is a true family. It is a manifestation on earth of the Divine Family of the Father, the Son, and the Holy Spirit.

In order for this not to become abstract, the Church expresses her familial place with God through a tangible series of ever-expanding bonds of love and commitment. The first and principal foundation of these relationships is holy matrimony.

As a point of emphasis, Saint Paul taught us how holy matrimony reflects the relationship between the Lord Jesus and his Church:

Be subject to one another out of reverence for Christ.

Wives, be subject to your husbands as you are to the Lord. For the husband is the head of the wife just as Christ is the head of the church, the body of which he is the Savior. Just as the church is subject to Christ, so also wives ought to be, in everything, to their husbands.

Husbands, love your wives, just as Christ loved the church and gave himself up for her, in order to make her holy by cleansing her with the washing of water by the word, so as to present the church to himself in splendor, without a spot or wrinkle or anything of the kind — yes, so that she may be holy and without blemish. In the same way, husbands should love their wives as they do their own bodies. He who loves his wife loves himself. For no one ever hates his own body, but he nourishes and tenderly cares for it, just as Christ does for the church, because we are members of his body. "For this reason a man will leave his father and mother and be joined to his wife, and the two will become one flesh." This is a great mystery, and I am applying it to Christ and the church. Each of you, however, should love his wife as himself, and a wife should respect her husband. (Ephesians 5:21–33)

Marriage is the bedrock upon which all the other relationships within the Church and society are bound and built. Any assault against marriage is an assault against the Church and the very fabric of society.

Family life is born from marriage and is the way in which we understand every other type of relationship. It is only from the immediate family of husband, wife, and children that we can realize and value other familial relationships. It is only through the Christian family that we can begin to understand the Church herself as a family.

Saint Paul stressed the importance of family life. He taught us that every family is gathered together and named by God himself. "For this reason I bow my knees before the Father, from whom every family in heaven and on earth takes its name" (Eph 3:14–15). The passing on of the Faith comes through the family. Each family member has his or her part to play in giving witness and instruction to the young Christian who is being formed and taught the way of the Lord Jesus. The family is assisted by the local community of faith.

Becoming a godparent is an incorporation into your godchild's family. If you are already related to your godchild, becoming a godparent deepens and enhances your relationship in a profound way. This is an act of God, which Christian parents and families should honor and appreciate. No godparent should be treated like an outsider, and godparents, for their part, should not allow themselves to become strangers. Godparents are an important part of the Christian family.

The Bond of Charity

Believing needs belonging, and young Christians need an entire extended family and local parish in order to receive the Faith and grow into discipleship. The *Catechism* emphasizes this point:

> Baptism is the sacrament of faith. But faith needs the community of believers. It is only within the faith of the Church that each of the faithful can believe. The faith required for Baptism is not a perfect and mature faith, but a beginning that is called to develop. The catechumen or the godparent is asked: "What do you ask of God's Church?" The response is: "Faith!" (1253)

In this way, we truly see and experience the Church as the family of God. It is our spiritual family, the place where we love God and learn about him. It is where we learn to love one another as Jesus Christ loves us. Saint Paul exhorts us:

> Let love be genuine; hate what is evil, hold fast to what is good; love one another with mutual affection; outdo one another in showing honor. Do not lag in zeal, be ardent in spirit, serve the Lord. Rejoice in hope, be patient in suffering, persevere in prayer. Contribute to the needs of the saints; extend hospitality to strangers.
>
> Bless those who persecute you; bless and do

> not curse them. Rejoice with those who rejoice, weep with those who weep. Live in harmony with one another; do not be haughty, but associate with the lowly; do not claim to be wiser than you are. Do not repay anyone evil for evil, but take thought for what is noble in the sight of all. If it is possible, so far as it depends on you, live peaceably with all. (Romans 12:9–18)

This is the bond of charity that we learn and live within the Church, the family of God.

As a godparent, you are a part of your godchild's extended family. God's providence has put you in this unique place of service, and you are called to give witness to the Faith and live a life of loving service to others. In this way, you help build up the Body of Christ and show the Church to be the family of God.

As the family of God, the Church's unity transcends all earthly things, from socioeconomic status, language, and citizenship to personality and politics — and even to time and space. Yes, even time and space are creatures that have no power over the bond of charity lived among baptized Christians. This is deeply encouraging especially for those who live far away from their godchildren but still want to play a role in their lives.

The Body of Christ is invigorated by the Holy Spirit, and nothing — not even death — can divide the body. As Saint Paul teaches us: "For as in one body we have many members, and not all the members have the same function, so we, who are many, are one body in Christ, and individually we are members one of another" (Rom 12:4–5).

As members of the Body of Christ, we have shared blessings and graces between us. We also have particular opportunities and responsibilities to one another. These sacred duties include praying for one another, giving witness and encouragement in our mutual needs, and selflessly serving one another in the Lord's name.

These sacred duties are the responsibility of every Christian, but especially those who have a specific call from God, such as parents and godparents. Such sacred duties must thrive in this life and continue on into eternal life. Death has no power over the family of God. The grave does not conclude the sacred duties we owe to one another.

Eternal Life

Baptism is about new life. Here in this life, we begin to experience this new life in Jesus Christ, and we will experience it fully in eternity. Since baptism is about eternal life, the call of the godparent is uniquely tied to the promise and hope for heaven. As a godparent, you thus stand as a witness to your godchild of the extended family in the Church, both those living on earth and those who have died. You testify to the reality and importance of the Communion of Saints.

What does this mean?

In his public ministry, the Lord Jesus quoted from the lineage of the Old Testament and identified God as the

God of Abraham, Isaac, and Jacob. He told us, "[God] is not the God of the dead, but of the living" (Mk 12:27). The patriarchs of old, though they died, live on in eternity, and the Lord points to them as models of what it means to dwell with God forever.

In similar fashion, within the Body of Christ, we turn to all the saints, the friends of God, who are our brothers and sisters in heaven. We ask them for guidance, encouragement, and prayer. As on earth, so in heaven. We are one Body, united to one another in Jesus Christ.

Everyone in heaven is a saint, including not only the canonized saints of the Church, but also those holy ones who are known only to us and our families. We are united to those in heaven, for the admonition of Saint Peter does not end at death: "Finally, all of you, have unity of spirit, sympathy, love for one another, a tender heart, and a humble mind" (1 Pt 3:8). We follow his guidance by turning to the saints and asking for their help. They offer us their intercession and friendship.

In addition to the holy ones in heaven, we also pray for those who have recently died and all those who might still be in the process of purgation as the Lord Jesus prepares them for heaven. It is a noble thing to pray and offer sacrifice for the souls in purgatory, and it is a praiseworthy practice to teach young Christians to do the same.

We remember our beloved dead; we pray for them, share stories about them, visit their earthly resting places, and remember them at the altar during the Mass. In this way, we display our union with the Lord Jesus and with one another. We show by our way of life here that there is a communion among all the baptized, both living and dead.

In your unique relationship with your godchild, you have a special call to exemplify the fullness of Christian communion, and to nurture your godchild's awareness of the Communion of Saints. You can do this through prayer, through example, and even through the things you choose to discuss and the resources and gifts you share with your godchild.

United in Prayer

Christian life and prayer is a communal affair. It involves the entire People of God, both in heaven and on earth. And so, no Christian ever walks or prays alone.

In addition to our family ties here on earth, we are also united with a "great cloud of witnesses" as the Letter to the Hebrews teaches us:

> Therefore, since we are surrounded by so great a cloud of witnesses, let us also lay aside every weight and the sin that clings so closely, and let us run with perseverance the race that is set before us, looking to Jesus the pioneer and perfecter of our faith, who for the sake of the joy that was set before him endured the cross, disregarding its shame, and has taken his seat at the right hand of the throne of God. (12:1–2)

From the perspective of eternity, our prayers on earth unite us with the Blessed Virgin Mary and all the angels and saints. The entire heavenly court is involved in the prayers we offer throughout our lives. Our prayers are united to theirs. We are one people, one body, one family in God. As such, we are called to the same way of life. Saint Peter exhorts us: "Honor everyone. Love the family of believers. Fear God. Honor the emperor" (1 Pt 2:17).

In addition to praying with us, the saints in heaven serve as our guides for growth in holiness. They can teach and direct us in the interior life. If you want to be a great godparent, get to know the saints. They will inspire and help you in your own discipleship and support you as you pray for and accompany your godchild. Then, you will be well equipped to teach your godchild about the saints and encourage him or her to pray to them often.

The *Catechism* explains:

> The witnesses who have preceded us into the kingdom, especially those whom the Church recognizes as saints, share in the living tradition of prayer by the example of their lives, the transmission of their writings, and their prayer today" (2683).

In one brief but powerful sentence, we have a complete summary of the contributions of the great witnesses of the kingdom to our lives and to the spiritual treasury of the Church.

First, the witnesses have run the race of this life and received their crown. They fought the good fight and won their victory in Jesus Christ. They have received the Beatific Vision and are rejoicing in God's presence. They have a front-row seat in heaven and are sharing a union with God in which our prayer on earth seeks to participate.

Second, while this is especially true of those who are canonized saints, it also includes all the holy ones in heaven. Everyone in heaven is a saint, and so every saint — canonized or not — can be a witness to us of the power of spending time with God.

Third, the saints share in the living tradition of prayer by the example of their lives. They prayed, and that example shines out and convicts us in this life to pray as they prayed.

Fourth, those saints who left us writings on the spiritual life contribute to the living tradition by their writings, mystical accounts, insights, and instructions.

Fifth, the saints are not dead people who have no voice and play no part in the life of the Church today. Quite the opposite. The cloud of witnesses is active and interceding for the Church today. The saints are not remote models that we stare at and emulate in some distant fashion. The saints are here and an active part of our lives. They live with God and with us. They are more alive now than they ever have been, and they want to come and share that abundant life with us. The witnesses want to accompany us and actively encourage us to seek a life in

God above all things.

In reference to these witnesses, the *Catechism* powerfully tells us that they "contemplate God, praise him and constantly care for those whom they have left on earth. When they entered into the joy of their Master, they were 'put in charge of many things'" (2683). The saints in heaven remember us, call to us, and want to guide us to union with God. The thick veil of death has not removed them from us. They are among us and keep pointing us to the things of God. They call us to pray, and they offer to pray for us. They intercede for us and desire to teach us about the ways of God.

The *Catechism* makes the urgent point: "Their intercession is their most exalted service to God's plan. We can and should ask them to intercede for us and for the whole world" (2683).

As a godparent, you can make it a daily practice to direct the soul of your godchild to these great witnesses and masters of the spiritual life. There is no greater teaching or service that we can give than to teach another person how to encounter God. As godparents, the greatest service we can render our godchildren is providing them a robust example of the spiritual life and a strong formation in the ways of prayer, always looking to the saints in heaven for guidance and help.

Key Takeaways

- ➡ The Church is the family of God, and we see

and experience this familial identity in different relationships, including relationships with our godparents.

- ➡ Holy matrimony is the first and principal relationship in the Church and society, from which flows the immediate family and then the extended family.
- ➡ Godparents are a part of their godchild's extended family, even if they are not related by blood.
- ➡ The family of God includes the saints in heaven and the souls in purgatory, to whom we are united by the bond of charity and joined through prayer.
- ➡ Godparents have an important duty to support Christian parents in exemplifying and teaching young Christians how to pray and to navigate the spiritual life, looking in a special way to the example and help of the saints in heaven.

Spiritual Resources and Practices

- Pray to Our Lady and ask for a greater awareness and acceptance of your status as a member of your godchild's extended family. Make resolutions to spiritually strengthen this bond of charity.

- Discuss your status as extended family member with the Christian parents of your godchild and make concrete plans with them to preserve and build up this bond as the years go by.
- Pray the Litany of the Saints for (and, if possible, with) your godchild.
- Pray a decade of the Glorious Mysteries of the Rosary for the deceased members of your godchild's family.
- When possible, attend the funeral Masses of people in your godchild's family.

Pray the following prayers for your godchild:

An Act of Hope

O Lord God,
I hope by your grace for the pardon
of all my sins
and after life here to gain eternal happiness
because you have promised it
who are infinitely powerful, faithful, kind,
and merciful.
In this hope I intend to live and die.
Amen.

The Magnificat

My soul proclaims the greatness of the Lord,
my spirit rejoices in God my Savior,
for he has looked with favor on his humble
servant.
From this day all generations will call me blessed,
the Almighty has done great things for me,
and holy is his Name.
He has mercy on those who fear Him
in every generation.
He has shown the strength of his arm,
he has scattered the proud in their conceit.
He has cast down the mighty from their
thrones
and has lifted up the humble.
He has filled the hungry with good things,
and the rich he has sent away empty.
He has come to the help of his servant Israel
for he has remembered his promise of mercy,
the promise he made to our fathers,
to Abraham and his children forever.

Guardian Angel Prayer

Angel of God, my guardian dear,
to whom God's love commits me here,
ever this day be at my side,

to light and guard, to rule and guide.
Amen.

Possible Activities

- Go to Mass on the feast of All Saints or All Souls and pray for your godchild. If possible, attend Mass with your godchild and his or her family. If this isn't possible, make time to talk with your godchild about why these holy days are important. Discuss the connection between baptism and eternal life.
- Give your godchild an age-appropriate book on the lives of the saints. If possible, read and learn about some of the saints together, especially ones that neither of you recognize, as well as your godchild's patron saint (which can be based on name or your godchild's personal choice).
- If you are able to spend time with your godchild and his or her family in person, visit a local parish church together and talk about the saints depicted in its statues and stained-glass windows or other artwork. Or consider visiting a cemetery or columbarium together and praying for the dead.

Chapter Four

The Ministry of Accompaniment

The Lord is my shepherd, I shall not want.
He makes me lie down in green pastures;
he leads me beside still waters;
he restores my soul.
He leads me in rights paths
for his name's sake.

— Psalm 23:1–3

As Christians, we walk with the Lord Jesus on his way. We accompany and help one another on the journey. The ministry of accompaniment is embedded in the very life of the Christian believer. It finds a heightened expression in certain callings, such as holy matrimony, Christian parenthood, and serving as a godparent.

Years ago, one of the young women in my parish introduced me to an older woman who was visiting her family for her high school graduation. She was excited for me to meet her guest. She happily told me that older woman was her godmother. As the young woman was sharing who the older woman was, she began to cry and couldn't finished her sentences.

I realized there was something more behind the relationship, and I waited to discover what it was.

It took the young woman a few tries before she could finish her thought. She told me, "This is my godmother. She's always been there. When I was a freshman, there was a lot of bullying. People were making fun of my weight. I didn't know what to do about it and so I started ... well, I got stuck in an eating disorder. No one noticed, except her. She asked me how things were going at school. She knew how to ask. And she listened to me."

The older woman stood there, composed but with a quivering lip. It was clear she was holding back some emotions.

"My godmother listened to me," the young woman continued. "It took a while but eventually I told her what was happening. She didn't judge me. She helped me talk to my parents and get help."

At this point, both women were crying, and their mutual love and respect was palpable.

The young woman spoke again, "I'm so glad she could come and be here for my graduation. I don't know what I would have done without her."

I felt honored to share in that moment and grateful that the young woman felt comfortable sharing such a personal part of her life. I don't think she realized how transparent she was being, since her focus was on expressing her gratitude to her godmother.

This is a powerful story of a godmother who played her part and fulfilled her sacred duty. This is a godmother who understood the summons to guide and accompany her goddaughter.

While the service of a godparent will be expressed in a variety of different ways, they all converge and are expressed in a sincere love and faithful accompaniment through life. As a further illustration of accompaniment, and as a way for us to go deeper in our understanding of what it means to walk together along the way of the Lord Jesus, we will consider three separate events from Scripture: two from the life of the Lord and one from the accounts of the early Church.

Being a Simon of Cyrene

Every godparent is called to the specific ministry of accompaniment. This ministry has its quiet and peaceful days, but also its turbulent and arduous days. Walking with another person means helping them carry whatever God's providence sends their way. In some instances, God's active will sends joys and triumphs. It is important to rejoice in these moments and to share in the celebrations that surround them. In other instances, God's permissive will allows for sorrows and struggles. It is important to embrace these moments and help our godchild carry any crosses God allows.

No person chooses how he will walk the way of the Lord. The Lords gives us what he wills. In similar fashion, no faithful companion of another person gets to choose how and when to walk with another person. Accompaniment is about consistency, faithfulness, and reliability.

Jesus himself had many companions during his earthly life. Of course, the apostles accompanied him in his three-year public ministry. But in one of his greatest hours of need, an unexpected companion was sent to the Lord. During his passion, when his closest friends had abandoned him, a man named Simon was seized and ordered to help the Lord carry his cross: "As they led him away, they seized a man, Simon of Cyrene, who was coming from the country, and they laid the cross on him, and made him carry it behind Jesus" (Lk 23:26).

The man was from Cyrene in North Africa. He did not know the Lord Jesus beforehand, but he was thrust into a powerful moment of accompaniment. Perhaps unwillingly at first, Simon fulfilled his call with great dedication. As such, he stands as a model for everyone who is called to accompany another in suffering.

God's permissive will allows for crosses in the lives of his children, just as he permitted the cross in the life of his divine Son. Every cross is a moment of grace. Every cross has a lesson. Every cross is an opportunity to live our baptismal graces by dying to ourselves and living completely for Jesus Christ.

The person who is called to accompany another, especially a godparent, must be willing to help the other person to carry the crosses that God's providence allows them. There is no room for fair weather companions. The cross lies at the heart of the call to walk with another and accompany him or her through life.

As a godparent, you must understand this call to a ministry of accompaniment. It means willingly embracing every part of this call, which includes walking with your godchild through the sufferings and difficulties of life.

In our desire to accompany and to serve, we have to make sure we preserve the role of Simon of Cyrene, which is helping another person to carry his or her own cross. The cross is that person's to bear. It is not our cross. We have to be cautious of imitating another Simon mentioned in the Scriptures:

> Now a certain man named Simon had previously practiced magic in the city and amazed the people of Samaria, saying that he was someone great. Now when Simon saw that the Spirit was given through the laying on of the apostles' hands, he offered them money, saying, "Give me also this power so that anyone on whom I lay my hands may receive the Holy Spirit." But Peter said to him, "May your silver perish with you, because you thought you could ob-

> tain God's gift with money! You have no part or share in this, for your heart is not right before God. Repent therefore of this wickedness of yours, and pray to the Lord that, if possible, the intent of your heart may be forgiven you."
> (Acts of the Apostles 8:9, 18–22)

Unlike Simon of Cyrene, who helped the Lord Jesus to carry his cross, Simon the Magician wanted to buy what was not his. He sought to purchase the power of God to minister to other people for his own gain.

As we accompany others, we cannot snatch and grab the cross of another. The cross that God gives to one soul is not meant for another. As we accompany our godchild in carrying the cross, we have to remember that our godchild's cross is not ours. And any help we may offer is not ours, either. We are God's ministers. We share what we have been given — not for our own gain, but for love of God and our godchild.

The sufferings and sorrows of our life have all been arranged by God's benevolent providence. He does not desire these sufferings in themselves, but he does permit them for our good. They are the means by which we work out our salvation in Jesus Christ. As difficult as it can be to suffer or to watch those we love suffer, we must respect boundaries and help where we can, while striving to honor the other person and the crosses that belong to him or her.

We can walk this way with confidence, for, "We

know that all things work together for good for those who love God, who are called according to his purpose" (Rom 8:28).

As a godparent, you have been called to accompany your godchild through life, which will sometimes mean serving as a Simon of Cyrene, helping your godchild carry the cross with trust.

Our Emmaus Walk

While the harder moments of accompaniment will come, most of your role as a godparent will involve the more ordinary and general expression of accompaniment. As an example of this kind of accompaniment, we will explore the accompaniment of the Risen Christ with two of his disciples on the road to Emmaus.

In many respects, this scene from the Gospel illustrates what godparents are called to be and to do in the life of their godchildren. Saint Luke recounts:

> Now on that same day two of them were going to a village called Emmaus, about seven miles from Jerusalem, and talking with each other about all these things that had happened. While they were talking and discussing, Jesus himself came near and went with them, but their eyes were kept from recognizing him. And he said to them, "What are you discussing with each other while you walk along?" They stood still, looking sad. Then one of them, whose name was Cleop-

> as, answered him, "Are you the only stranger in Jerusalem who does not know the things that have taken place there in these days?" He asked them, "What things?" They replied, "The things about Jesus of Nazareth, who was a prophet mighty in deed and word before God and all the people, and how our chief priests and leaders handed him over to be condemned to death and crucified him. But we had hoped that he was the one to redeem Israel. Yes, and besides all this, it is now the third day since these things took place." Then he said to them, "Oh, how foolish you are, and how slow of heart to believe all that the prophets have declared! Was it not necessary that the Messiah should suffer these things and then enter into his glory?" Then beginning with Moses and all the prophets, he interpreted to them the things about himself in all the scriptures. (Luke 24:13–21, 25–27)

The account of the two disciples on the way to Emmaus is a treasure chest of divine truths. It teaches us (and reminds us) of the Lord's initiative toward each of us. The account helps us to understand the presence and goodness of the Risen Christ as he accompanies and transforms confused, scared, and distracted disciples into zealous heralds of his Gospel. The Lord turns sorrowful hearts into strong hearts, which then burn with confidence in him.

Truth be told, the two disciples had given up. We are told they were leaving the holy city of Jerusalem. They wanted to leave everything they knew about the Lord Jesus behind them. They were leaving the holy city in desolation, saying, "We thought that he was going to be the one." They had lost their confidence in the Lord. They had no hope, no faith, no willingness to hear the testimony or to believe in the power of the Resurrection.

The two disciples were so distracted in their disappointment that they couldn't see the mighty works that were already happening in Jerusalem. They could not recognize Jesus when he began to accompany them.

In our lives, we can also get distracted by our own emotions, disappointments, sorrows, loneliness, and anxiety. These can become so consuming that we can't even see the mighty works that God his doing right in front of us.

We have to allow ourselves to have eyes of faith. Then, we need to share that faith with others.

The two disciples had abandoned belief in the Lord Jesus, yet he sought them out. What a powerful display of love! The Lord went to them, searched for them, sought to walk with them. He began a journey with them. The Lord Jesus is a true companion who diligently accompanies us even when we are not aware.

The Lord seeks us out, even in our darkest hours. While we can be unfaithful, he is always faithful to us. He wants to journey with us. He wants to walk with us, to be a part of our lives and make us strong. He seeks to fill us up with immense hope and a zealous sense of mission. As the Lord ministers to us and accompanies us, he simultaneously models for us how we are to minister to and accompany one another.

As the two disciples reached Emmaus, they asked the Lord to stay with them, since the night was coming. The Lord, who had sought them out and taught them, was now being sought out. Their hearts had been converted. They had been given new strength. With their hearts now burning, they said to Jesus, "Stay with us" (Acts 24:29).

As we seek to live in peace, this should be the petition of our hearts: "Lord, stay with me. Help me!" Such a petition nurtures and fuels our spirits. The disciples asked, and the Lord Jesus stayed. Then he disappeared from their presence after the Breaking of the Bread.

As he disappeared, the disciples were reborn and ran to Jerusalem to announce what had happened to them. They were new creations. Their sorrow had given way to purpose.

As they arrived and told the account of the Lord's presence with them, the Gospel tells us: "While they were still speaking about this, Jesus himself stood in their midst and said to them, 'Peace be with you'" (Acts 24:36).

The joy and mission of the two disciples is now shared with the entire Christian community. Their account shows us that the heaviness and hardships of our lives are not the end, and they do not define us. Try as they might, they do not define our world. The sorrows and sufferings of the world have no real power over us.

We will walk through this valley of the shadow of darkness, knowing that the Risen Christ, the strong and powerful Lord, is with us, guiding us and giving us his strength. As he gives us his strength, we are called to give that strength to others. As the Lord humbles himself and walks with us, we are called to die to ourselves and faithfully walk with others. This is the summons of every Christian, especially a godparent to a godchild.

Five Important Lessons

Saint Luke is the one who recorded the famed Emmaus account for us. He was hailed as the "beloved physician" and is the only Gentile author of the New Testament.

Saint Luke was in the second generation of the Lord's disciples, and he most likely never met Jesus Christ in this life. And yet, drawing from the apostolic testimony, Saint Luke gives us the expansive account of the Risen Christ accompanying, listening to, teaching, praying, and breaking bread with two of his disciples.

For these reasons, the Emmaus account is one of the most beloved narratives within the Christian community. Even after two thousand years of reflection and commentary, the possible interpretations and applications of this Resurrection account are endless.

Godparents, in particular, can draw much wisdom from the rich spiritual and exegetical patrimony of this account. This wisdom will shed some light on what it means for us to support, journey, and accompany others, especially our godchildren, along the way of the Lord.

The disciples on the road to Emmaus were downcast and struggling with spiritual desolation. They had been awaiting the restoration of David's kingdom, and the work of the Lord didn't go the way they had hoped. They were confused, anxious, and — in light of their abrupt response to the Lord: "Are you the only stranger in Jerusalem who does not know the things that have taken place there in these days?" — it appears they were a little on edge. Things were not going the way they had expected.

And yet, the Lord was there with them. He entered into their state of uncertainty and frustration. They just didn't see him at first.

In our lives, we can focus on our disappointments and sufferings. We can become restless and angry. We can imagine that God is not with us and has abandoned us in our time of need. And yet, the Lord is with us. He is accompanying us and suffering with us, and he wants us to talk with him about what's happening. He invites us to welcome him as an active sojourner in our lives.

As the Lord listens and walks with us, we are called to listen and walk with others. Godparents are especially called to listen and walk with their godchildren.

After an initial inquiry, the Lord realized that the disciples did not understand the role of suffering and why it was "necessary that the Christ should suffer." In response, the Lord opened the Scriptures and began to teach them. The Bible was the Lord's "go to" resource to share divine wisdom and to reveal the plan of salvation.

In our lives, the Lord wants us to understand how our suffering can be redemptive. He shows us how our tribulations and sufferings can be offered up for a greater good. The Lord calls us to open our Bibles and read them. He wants to instruct us in the same way as he taught the two disciples on the way to Emmaus. If offered up in the Lord, our sufferings can prove an amazingly blessed opportunity to draw close to the Lord. Our sufferings point us to the Bible and call us to encounter God and seek a greater understanding of suffering.

As we learn about suffering and are enlightened and instructed through the Bible, so we are called to teach others about suffering, opening the Scriptures and helping others see divine wisdom in difficult circumstances. Godparents, in particular, are called to instruct their godchildren in the ways of suffering and help them to understand the Bible as the Word of God.

After the Lord Jesus taught the two disciples, they arrived in Emmaus. It was beginning to be nightfall, and the disciples asked him, "Stay with us, because it is almost evening and the day is now nearly over" (Acts 24:29). The Lord agreed and stayed with them.

As a godparent, reflect on this reality: In your life, do you call out for divine assistance? Do you pray, "Lord, it's getting dark. Help me!"? If we open the door to him, then the Lord will come in and dispel our darkness. He will recline with us and become a part of our family. But we have to welcome him.

As we welcome the Lord, we are also called to open our hearts to others. Godparents should always have open hearts to our godchildren. If your godchild calls out for help, you should be ready to answer.

Lastly, as the Lord joined his disciples for a meal, he broke bread and was manifested to them. In that Eucharistic act, the disciples realized that it was the Lord Jesus who was with them, and they rejoiced. This is an invitation to reflect: Are we truly hungry for holy Communion? We can beseech the Lord to reveal himself to us in the Mass and ask him to help us understand that his own Body and Blood are true food and true drink.

As the Lord Jesus draws close to us in the Mass and in holy Communion, we are called to draw close to one another. As the Lord feeds us, we are called to feed one another. Take some time to consider: How can you strengthen your attentiveness to the spiritual and emotional needs of your godchild? What can you do to encourage your godchild to regularly attend Mass and receive holy Communion worthily? Do you speak often of the Lord's presence in the Eucharist?

For godparents, the Emmaus account serves as a guide for our call to accompany our godchildren and their families in the joys and sorrows of life. This account offers a summary — almost point by point — of how we should accompany and serve our godchildren in their own journeys of discipleship.

The Example of Priscilla and Aquila

After looking at the example of Simon of Cyrene and the account of the road to Emmaus, we must consider another aspect of accompaniment: the moments when we will be called to offer instruction, guidance, and sometimes gentle correction.

Of course, we are all perpetual students. We are all works in progress. As disciples, our journey is a lifelong adventure of constant conversion, instruction, and renewal. As godparents, we should not shy away from being corrected or guided to a fuller understanding of the Gospel. And we should not avoid giving such guidance and correction when necessary, always relying on God's grace and the guidance of the Holy Spirit.

In the Acts of the Apostles, we hear about a very learned young man named Apollos. He studied in the northern African city of Alexandria, a major center of education in the ancient world. He had studied the Sacred Scriptures there, since the School of Alexandria had a highly developed approach to the Bible and the various ways of interpreting it.

Apollos was already a believer. He already knew the way of the Lord Jesus and was eager to teach and preach about Jesus Christ. On one occasion, Apollos went to Ephesus and began to preach "with burning enthusiasm," speaking "boldly" (Acts 18:25, 26).

In the synagogue where Apollos preached, there was a holy married couple, Priscilla and Aquila. This couple was very dear to Saint Paul and an essential part of his missionary outreach.

Aquila is believed to have been one of the seventy original disciples of the Lord Jesus. Saint Paul met the holy couple in Corinth when they fled Italy under the Emperor Claudius (Acts 18:1–3). He began to work with them because they, like him, were tentmakers by trade. He stayed in their home, which became an early center for the Faith (see 1 Cor 16:19). Later, Priscilla and Aquila traveled with Paul when he left Corinth. They were loyal to the Gospel and risked their lives in support of Saint Paul (Rom 16:3–4).

When Priscilla and Aquila heard Apollos preach, they were impressed since he "taught accurately the things concerning Jesus" but they realized that he needed further guidance because "he knew only the baptism of John" (Acts 24: 25, 26). Saint Luke recounts:

> Now there came to Ephesus a Jew named Apollos, a native of Alexandria. He was an eloquent man, well-versed in the scriptures. He had been instructed in the Way of the Lord; and he spoke with burning enthusiasm and taught accurately the things concerning Jesus, though he knew only the baptism of John. He began to speak boldly in the synagogue; but when Priscilla and Aquila heard him, they took him aside and explained the Way of God to him more accurately. (Acts of the Apostles 18:24–26)

While Priscilla and Aquila were not the godparents of Apollos, they certainly fulfilled the spiritual role of godparents. We're told that the holy couple took Apollos aside and explained the Way of the Lord "more accurately" to him. The husband and wife took the time to listen, make some mental notes, meet with Apollos personally, and teach him. In many respects, we can see Priscilla and Aquila as the patron saints of godparents!

In collaborating with the Christian parents, there will be times when we will need to provide guidance and instruction to our godchildren. Godparents should know the teachings of the Lord Jesus and the Church well and be able to explain them and answer any questions our godchildren might have about them.

While the situations in which godparents will need to teach can be vast and distinct, here are some more common ones you may face:

- Your godchild has not been well formed in the Faith and needs more teaching. In this scenario, you should gently seek to supplement what is spiritually lacking in the mind and heart of your godchild, coordinating your efforts with your godchild's parents, provided they are living the Faith themselves.
- Your godchild has been influenced by another spiritual or religious tradition and doesn't "want to be Catholic anymore." In this situation, your role as a godparent is to

listen and discreetly introduce some basic apologetics — the defense of Catholic doctrines through discussions about the Faith, explaining its beliefs. While you may not be able to change your godchild's mind in the moment, you can at least plant important and lasting seeds.

- Your godchild no longer believes in God. In this situation, a more spiritual response is needed. Gently introduce prayer and spiritual practices to your godchild before attempting to introduce some general apologetics to help them see that belief in God is reasonable.
- Your godchild has undergone a deeper conversion and wants to know more about the Faith. In this scenario, you should introduce spiritual and catechetical resources, but also cooperate with your godchild's parents to help your godchild exercise prudence and caution in the midst of newfound zeal and excitement.
- Your godchild undergoes a great tragedy, loss, or heartbreak and doesn't understand why God has let it happen. In this situation, you are called to listen and accompany in silence. Only after the initial shock has lessened should you offer any spiritual explanations.

- Your godchild has begun to engage in immoral actions (which might include vandalism, bullying, viewing pornography, fornication, smoking marijuana, drinking, or using other drugs, etc.) and believes these actions are not problematic. When possible, you should work closely with your godchild's parents, seeking an opportunity to compassionately name the sin and its consequences and show your godchild the most excellent way of the Lord Jesus.

In each of these situations, and countless more, your accompaniment as a godparent will be expressed in giving instruction, encouragement, spiritual direction, guidance, and gentle, loving correction. In any situation that arises, you are called to realize your sacred duty and responsibility to give witness to the Faith and to teach your godchild the way of true Christian discipleship.

See yourself before the throne of God and recommit yourself to the Lord Jesus and his Gospel every day. Ask him to strengthen your personal discipleship and to give you the grace you need to be a faithful witness to the godchild he has entrusted to your care. For truly, there is no greater love that can be given to another person than to bear witness to Jesus Christ, "the way, and the truth, and the life" (Jn 14:6).

Key Takeaways

- ➡ The vocation of a godparent is a ministry of faith and accompaniment.
- ➡ Godparents have a special duty to help their godchildren carry the crosses in their lives, imitating Simon of Cyrene, who helped Jesus carry his cross.
- ➡ As seen in the Emmaus account, the Lord walks with us and accompanies us through life, and all of us — but godparents in a special way — are called to imitate him by accompanying one another.
- ➡ Priscilla and Aquila, who accompanied Apollos by instructing and correcting him in the Faith, can be seen as special patron saints of godparents.
- ➡ In collaboration with the Christian parents, godparents are to teach, guide, and offer gentle correction to their godchild in the ways of faith.

Spiritual Resources and Practices

- Read the Acts of the Apostles and note the different examples of accompaniment from the various stories of the saints in the life of the early Church.

- Study the life of Priscilla and Aquila (they are mentioned in Acts 18:2–3, 18, and 26, and in Rom 16:3–4, 1 Cor 16:19, and 2 Tm 4:19) and note some specific ways you can model your ministry as a godparent on their holy example.
- Make spiritual reading a regular practice for yourself, including the Bible, the *Catechism*, and books on spirituality, basic doctrine, and apologetics.
- Pray the Divine Mercy Chaplet on Fridays for the final perseverance of your godchild.
- Regularly entrust your godchild to the Sacred Heart of Jesus.

Pray the following prayers for your godchild:

An Act of Love

O Lord God, I love you above all things
and I love my neighbor for your sake
because you are the highest, infinite and perfect
good, worthy of all my love.
In this love I intend to live and die.
Amen.

Prayer to Mother Mary for Protection

We fly to your protection, most holy Mother of God; please listen to our petitions and needs, and deliver us from all dangers, ever glorious and blessed Virgin Mary.

Mary, our model and mother, by your obedience and patience you have taught us how to be true children of God. Please help us by your powerful assistance to overcome all our weaknesses, and to fulfill perfectly our tasks in life.

By your compassionate aid may we ever stand in spirit with you beneath the cross of Christ so that we may also rejoice with you in your divine Son's triumphant victory over sin and death.

In your maternal kindness help us to be faithful to prayers in the company of God's Church as you were one with the Apostles in the Upper Room as you waited for the promised Spirit of Pentecost.

With your gracious assistance may we be near you in the glory of Christ's kingdom and come to sing with you and all the faithful the eternal praise of God. Amen.

Lead: O Mary, conceived without sin,
Response: Pray for us who have recourse to you.

Guardian Angel Prayer

Angel of God, my guardian dear,
to whom God's love commits me here,
ever this day be at my side,
to light and guard, to rule and guide.
Amen.

Possible Activities

- Select a topic or theme (e.g., the Resurrection, the Communion of Saints, purgatory, the real presence of Jesus in the Eucharist) and have an open conversation with your godchild about it. If your godchild has questions about the Faith, introduce good Catholic resources for finding answers, including the *Catechism* and digital resources such as catholic.com (Catholic Answers), simplycatholic.com, and newadvent.org.
- Look for ways to express or highlight the Faith when you spend time with your godchild. For example, when you visit the zoo, talk about God's marvelous creation of the world. If you go fishing together, talk about

why the first apostles were fishermen. Use your imagination and be creative!

- Tell your godchild about your favorite story in the Gospels and spend some time discussing it together. Be open to any questions your godchild might have about Jesus and the stories of his life.
- Watch a movie about a saint or another holy, inspiring person with your godchild and talk about it. Discuss heroism and why the example of holy people matters so much.

Conclusion

When I was in the seminary, as my class was preparing for priestly ordination, I mentioned that my godparents were going to come to my ordination and that my godfather was going to serve as one of the lectors at my First Mass. Many of my classmates didn't even know who their godparents were. Some speculated that they thought it was their aunt and uncle, while others were just dismissive, saying things like, "I think my godparents were friends of my parents when I was a baby, but they don't keep in touch anymore."

This absence of godparents in my fellow seminarians' lives surprised me. It led me to a profound moment of gratitude for my own *padrinos*.

I've been blessed with good godparents, and so much of this book and its contents is the fruit of that great rapport and interaction that I — and my family —

have had with them through the years.

I hope more Christian children can experience this beautiful bond of connection with their own godparents. The Church is the family of God, and we need strong bonds that unite us, not only with our immediate families, but with the whole people of God.

We need a renewal in our understanding of godparents, and a strong affirmation of the role godparents are called to play in the lives of their godchildren and in the Church. Such a renewal begins with a deepening of the discernment process of Christian parents regarding whom they choose to ask to be godparents, why they choose them, and what expectations they have for prospective godparents.

It also requires that godparents discern their own role with more intention and seek to live it in concrete and meaningful ways. As we have explored in this book, godparents are called to a ministry of faith and accompaniment. That call is grounded within the very graces of baptism and the summons for all Christians to seek holiness.

If you are faithful to your call as a godparent, you can make a fundamental difference in the discipleship and spiritual growth of your godchild. Your witness and testimony of what it means to be a follower of Christ is sorely needed today. I pray that you will continue to grow as a disciple and to accompany your godchild on the journey of discipleship.

The way of the Lord Jesus is not easy, and we need

the support of others along the way. Godparents are meant to be a consolation, encouragement, and help through the ups and downs of life, not only for their godchildren, but for Christian parents and the whole Christian family.

I pray this book has helped develop your understanding of what it means to be godparent. I hope it has given some instruction and encouragement, perhaps ruffled some feathers, and provided you with sound and helpful ideas to help you be a loving, present, and faithful godparent. May this book serve as one small catalyst in the much-needed renewal and restoration of godparents as witnesses to the Faith, servants of the Gospel, and companions along the Way.

The LORD bless you and keep you;
the LORD make his face to shine upon you, and
be gracious to you;
the LORD lift up his countenance
upon you, and give you peace.

— Numbers 6:24–26

Daily Prayers for My Godchild

It is important that we pray daily for our godchildren. As sharers in the duty of forming new Christians and helping them along the way of the Lord, we are called to daily offer our godchildren to God and ask for his abundant blessings upon them.

To help you live this call, here are some suggested daily prayers.

Morning Offering

> O Jesus, through the Immaculate Heart of Mary, I offer you all my prayers, works, joys, and sufferings of this day, for all the intentions of your Sacred Heart, in union with the Holy Sacrifice of the Mass throughout the world, in reparation for my sins, for the intentions of my relatives and friends

(especially my godchild[ren], N), and in particular for the intentions of the Holy Father. Amen.

Prayer of Peace

Lord, make me an instrument of your peace:
where there is hatred, let me sow love;
where there is injury, pardon;
where there is doubt, faith;
where there is despair, hope;
where there is darkness, light;
where there is sadness, joy.
O divine Master, grant that I may
not so much seek
to be consoled as to console,
to be understood as to understand,
to be loved as to love.
For it is in giving that we receive,
it is in pardoning that we are pardoned,
and it is in dying that we are born to eternal
life. Amen.

Prayer to Our Lady of Good Counsel

Our Lady of Good Counsel, pray for us always; ask our God to help me and my godchild to be faithful to our baptism, to be fervent in prayer, and to be ready to live each day with your Son. Amen.

Sacred Moments in the Life of My Godchild

Name:

Date of Birth:

Patron Saint:

Sacraments

Holy Baptism:

First Confession:

First Holy Communion:

Confirmation:

Holy Matrimony:

Sacred Ordination/Religious Profession:

Anointing of the Sick:

Devotional Practices

Marian Consecration:

____

Brown Scapular Investiture:

____

First Retreat:

____

First Pilgrimage:

____

About the Author

Father Jeffrey Kirby, STD, is a Catholic priest, moral theologian, writer, and pastor of Our Lady of Grace Parish in Indian Land, South Carolina. He holds a doctorate in moral theology from the Holy Cross University in Rome. He is an adjunct professor of theology at Belmont Abbey College, a certified life coach, a radio personality, and a conference speaker, retreat master, and pilgrimage leader. In 2020, Father Kirby was appointed a Missionary of Mercy by Pope Francis. Father Kirby is a senior contributor to the Crux news site and is a frequent guest and the host of multiple miniseries on the Eternal Word Television Network (EWTN). He is a Papal Knight of the Holy Sepulcher and is an advocate for the Christians in the Holy Land.

OSV

You might also like:

Way of the Cross for Loved Ones Who Have Left the Faith

By Fr. Jeffrey Kirby, STD

When a loved one leaves the Catholic Faith, it can be devastating. Often, we feel helpless, unable to do anything to bring them back. Yet there is something we can do.

The best way to bring our loved ones back to the Faith is through prayer. In addition to invitations and conversations, we can't forget the power we have to pray for them. What better way to do that than by joining our fears and sufferings with those of Jesus in the Stations of the Cross?

In this book, the fourteen Stations have two emphases: intercession for loved ones and guidance for those still practicing the Faith. While contemplating our Savior's sacrificial love, readers of this devotional can intercede for friends and family as they spiritually carry the cross with Jesus, asking him to lead our loved ones back to fellowship with God and his Church.